# HER STORY

# HER STORY

## On Poetry, Pain, Love, Faith & Becoming

DAQUALA SHABRI HUNT

A Touch of Gold Art & Poetry

# CONTENTS

*This book is dedicated to you, may you never stop becoming the best version of yourself.*

*"You're not the best you're going to be but that's the nature of being creative. Everything you do should be an A minus, really good but there's still room for improvement."*

*-Eric "Ant Allik" Standifer*

First Printing, 2020

# FOREWORD

By: Lisa Murray

When DaQuala was 13 years old, her dream was to be an actress. One day as we were sight-seeing and appreciating the scenery we came to a bridge with a beautiful stream lined with rocks and water, DaQuala gasped with disbelief. Her disbelief was not at the beauty but it was an expression of disappointment and shame. She could not believe that we would waste water for selfish reasons when people are dying from thirst. It was then I knew that no matter what she did she would think about the needs of others. I knew she was destined for greatness.

As she experienced life and found ways to express her pain, fears, hopes, and dreams through art, performing, and writing she inspired me to explore myself. I know these poems were written as a part of her journey exploring the good, bad, and ugly of her inner most joys and pains not for herself but to inspire others. If you listen to the words of her poetry you may hear your voice, your cry, and find yourself as I have before.

## ~ I ~

# ON POETRY

Poetry came into her life at the young age of 10. She still remembers her first poem which was about love, since she has always been obsessed with romance. Her cousin Kim introduced her to poetry. Kim would write her own poems and share poetry books with her from authors who bared their hearts on paper. Since she looked up to Kim, anything Kim did she pretty much wanted to do so, she found her love for writing. Unfortunately, she lost her cousin to suicide in 2004. However, she did not lose what Kim taught her. Kim left her with poetry. She helped her find a voice. She helped her find a way to conceptualize her pain and to share her experiences. She used poetry to create stories, to share her own or bring light to others. Poetry became her lifeline and her eternal connection to Kim. Kim's essence is in every prose and rhyme.

To Kim, thank you for poetry.

-Her

# FOR KIM

Her truths were written
In prose and rhyme
She left her mark
in the sands of time
And I'd hope to learn
From her.
Learn how to turn
my pain into prose
Learn how to write freely
Turning my truths into poetry
She taught me how to accept me
How to be me unapologetically.
She made herself eternal
Words forever written
For generations to see.
Her poetry expressing her truth,
exposing the realities within me,
the realities within all of us.

# HER FIRST POEM

Do you love me?
I mean for real, do you?
You say you love me but
Do I know it's true?
When you see me,
you don't even hug me.
It's alright boo.
You know I'll always be there for you
No matter what we go through.
Mm, I guess I'm just in love with you.

# POETRY IS ALIVE

It's been a minute since I felt the power in my pen.
Poetry died in my heart, I guess this is a resurrection.
I've felt voiceless, never wanting loose lips,
only letting life flow from my ink tips.
A resurgence, a transference from my heart,
I'll let you in.
I've missed this.
Lately feeling like I've lost a piece of me.
I've needed the rhythm to send
electric shock waves into my body.
I've needed the rhythm to resuscitate me,
until my heart is beating poetry,
until my eyes are seeing poetry,
until my veins are bleeding poetry
until my lungs are breathing poetry.
Again.
That is poetry for me, very much alive.
And I guess it never died, I've just been without words.

# DESIRE TO WRITE

I had the desire to write.
And nothing or no one was going to stop me,
Not even myself.
Because sometimes, unknowingly,
I get in my own way.
I had the desire to scream,
To go crazy and let it all out.
I allowed myself to feel free... free from conformity
And instead of acting like everything was okay,
I allowed myself to transfer that energy.
I had the desire to laugh.
So, I surrounded myself with people I could laugh with,
I did not think about the negativity for once and I let go.
I laughed hysterically...for hours, until I got tired.
I had the desire to create.
My life is my masterpiece.
I want to leave a legacy and a lineage that will outlast
Every breath I have left on earth.
And I want my art to transform the minds
Of those around me.
I had the desire to love.
So, I opened up my heart to those who were most in need.
I allowed myself to love words that were pleasing to the ears.
I spent time with my family and friends, then
I let the Lord in, because I had the desire to be loved
And I needed to be loved by Him.

# BONDAGE OF TIME

I'm wrapped up in deadlines and due dates.
Tied down to clock ins and clock outs.
Institutionalized by time, captivating every part of me.
So much so I forget what I enjoy.
I'm staring at my laptop screen, anticipating
Hesitation keeps my hands above the keys
as I stare at the question "What makes you happy?"
Although happiness is only a state of being I sit here conflicted
Because it's not often I get to do what I enjoy.
Then I wonder: "Am I merely existing?"
I think of how often we get caught up with the ebbs and flow of life
Our happiness we often ignore.
"What makes you happy?" The question demands.
I remember...yeah, I used to love...
Wait, what did I used to love?
I used to love looking at the stars
Allowing their presence to light up my
heart with everlasting promises.
I used to love the kiss of fresh air as it eased its way through my lips
And filled my lungs with life.
Now as I walk out the door,
my only thoughts are about my daily routine.
My mind races ahead of me constantly
reminding me of my worries.

## LIFE AND DEATH IN THE TONGUE

**Her:**
I know he's cheating on me.
He's doing things more secretly.
On his phone constantly.
What the fuck is he hiding?
There has to be someone else
He always leaves me by myself
And when I ask to tag along
He always prefers to go alone
I believe the answers are in his phone
I'll scope it out to prove I'm wrong
And if I'm right he's dead to me
I'll take his breath, I'll watch him bleed
And I promise I'm not crazy
Just a broken-hearted lady
I find the messages, there's the proof
Secret meet ups with a woman, Jewel
Heat flushed my body, I begin to curse
Screaming at him the script I rehearsed
I can't believe he did this to me
I'll take his breath, I'll watch him bleed
Poison from the tongue of misery
A self-fulfilling prophecy
I'll never live happily
He didn't truly love me
Life and death in the tongue
I chose death to rule this one.

**Him:**
She's getting suspicious, I can tell
I hate keeping secrets, she knows me well.
She'll figure it out, ruin the surprise
That I'm planning for the
next step in our lives
The ring, the house,
I can't believe she's the one.
Although she can be crazy,
I know I'm done.
I'm meeting with the jeweler
tomorrow night is the night
That I ask my lady to be my wife
I hate that I'm lying,
but this has to go right
She's been through so much
She deserves the best life
Sleep comes over me
And I wake up to her screaming
She went through my phone
I must be dreaming
Yes, I've been hiding
Yes, I've been lying
But all for the surprise
I don't know what to tell her
Something's blinding her eyes
She can't see that I'm happy
that she's all that I need
Blinding insecurities making
her heart bleed.
Moments pass she's calm, I'm relieved.
Then she brings us a drink
She says sorry for flipping
And that she truly loves me
I'm sipping, I'm dying

I can no longer breathe.

# BLISS

My smile was filled with bliss,
that in hindsight I guess only ignorance could provide.
No, I can't do that, I can't deny
that I actually felt something real inside.
And in spite of my new-found knowledge I cannot pretend like
I didn't want our love to be one that would never end,
once upon a time.
But this is not a fairy tale and unfortunately
life does not always grant you with a happily ever after.
And although I wasn't expecting
our love to be this perfect masterpiece
I did not anticipate such a catastrophe.
And just in case you are not following me,
let me start from the beginning.
I noticed him before he noticed me.
I chuckled to myself when I caught him staring.
And He, was so handsome.
His demeanor emitted confidence and his smile
illuminated the room but I knew he could be
someone who damaged me if I wasn't careful.
A year went by after the exchange of our first hellos
which were followed by our first kiss,
our first I love you and our first argument.
And there were of course many times temptation would rise
but I didn't want sex to be our demise
because I've let sex ruin things in the past
and I wanted our love to be one that would last.
Plus, I knew the saying why buy the cow
when you can get the milk for free.

So. I wasn't giving him anything unless we were married.
See I am the type of woman that you put a ring on
...if you know what I mean.
And that's exactly what he did.
Everything was perfect, I was genuinely happy,
Even more so because we were loved by each other's families.
The pieces were coming together like perfect melodies
but I had no clue as to what was coming.
Looking back, I wish I would've asked why my mother was
staring so suspiciously at him when they first met.
But she never said anything so I pushed it aside
Hidden in the back of my mind... Until now.
And everything was great until everything went bad.
I was experiencing the greatest love I had ever had.
We decided it would be good if our families met
So, they could have a chance to interact.
My mother and sister, his parents and siblings
I thought everything was on the right track.
But everything was great until everything went bad.
My mom's best, baked lasagna, was brought in her hands,
smiles on our faces as I ushered her in.
My fiancé greeted me at the door with a simple kiss...
my life was filled with so much bliss.
And everything was great until
everything went BAD....
Lasagna painted the floor splattered with broken glass.
My father in law in shock,
My mother's sudden gasp.
And I'm nervous, as my mother repeatedly shakes her head no.
Images of this night I'll never let go.
And everything was great until everything went bad.
Before I could even ask, my mother had said,
I lied to you about your father,
He was never dead and you can't marry Michael,
his father is also your Dad.

# FRIEND ZONE

And my heart yearns to be loved by him,
In a way that'll make him say,
"I want to spend the rest of my life making you happy."
But still, I say nothing.
Instead, I continue to listen to his admirations
of different women who are not me.
I even give him advice on how to make them happy,
hiding my desires to be the one he can't stop thinking about.
Or that one who captivates his heart leaving him
paralyzed with just a heartbeat
I have to tell him.
I mean it shouldn't be that hard,
he's my best friend...I can tell him anything!
I'ma do it! I'm going to look him
dead in his eyes and say "I Love You"
And not in that Brown Sugar,
we're just friends, I love him like my brother type love.
But in that Love & Basketball,
"I'll play you for your heart," type of love.
But what if he doesn't feel the same?
And I ruin the very foundation of
how I fell in love with him in the first place.
That means no more movie nights, game nights,
or late-night conversations about breakups,
where we reassure each other it's alright.
But I can't take another moment of
my heart dropping to my stomach
because he's in love with another woman.
And I can't shake this feeling of hopelessness and regret

because he doesn't know that I am so
addicted to his smell that his scent is engrained
into the fibers of my brain
and each night I whisper his name in my sleep.
As fear builds in my mind I can't help but to be
nervous because our friendship is on the line.
And I wish my heart did not yearn for more
but I can't help that I fell in love with
how sweet his words sound in my ear.
Or how he would hold me like losing me was his biggest fear.
And now I'm sitting here, going back and forth between "what-ifs"
My mind going "Half Crazy" like Musiq because
my heart is oblivious to the fact that
our relationship has boundaries.
And I have to admit I'm scared because after I tell him,
there is no going back and if I lose him,
I am not prepared for that.
But it's time. I'm tired of waiting.
See, I heard you're supposed to marry your best friend
and I couldn't be closer to any other man.
So, I'm ready. It's time. I can do this! I just...have to.

# POETRY, DON'T LEAVE.

I've been looking for you.
It seems as if you've abandoned me.
I've been trying to find my reason to rhyme,
Have I lost it?
I've looked to the sky for inspiration.
I've tried to find creativity in the trees around me,
I meditated in a meadow of beautiful flowers
And still came up with nothing.
Where are you?
Through my pain you were obtainable but you
Appear to be non-existent in my peace.
Please...don't be fooled.
I still need you, poetry.
Stay with me.

# TESTIMONY OF A TEENAGER
## WRITTEN BY: KIMBERLY HUNT

Life is hard,
I can't explain why,
No one knows how hard I try.
When things are tough,
When life is bad,
I pretend that I am not sad.
I don't know how to let you know,
The pain I feel,
The hurt I don't show.

Life is hard,
Not yet for me,
Things that happen are meant to be.
I can't be happy every day,
But that doesn't mean,
That things aren't ok.
I don't crave attention,
I thrive by myself,
I am not always in need of your help.

Life is hard,
But things will be alright,
Now I can sleep through the night.
My life is on track,
The pieces are in place,
But I need my own time,
I need my own space.
I am different now,

I need you to see,
I am not anyone else,
I am just me.

# ~ II ~

## ON PAIN

The deepest pain she has felt has revolved around loss. Loss of a family member or loss of a relationship. Oftentimes she struggled with abandonment, wondering why it was easy for people to walk out of her life. She even got to a place where she expected it. However, the times she felt the most in pain was when she lost herself. That pain weighed her down. That pain led to more and more pain. Her brokenness attracted brokenness. She tried to find comfort in people, in "love", in sex, in avoiding, in everything else but God or through actually healing herself. She was walking in pain and she told no one, she just pretended to be okay. Jay-Z said, "You can't heal what you never reveal." If it was a physical ailment like a broken leg, she wouldn't just walk around like she felt nothing, she'd have a limp or hop. People would notice and ask what's wrong and hopefully make sure she sought outside support and resources to mend her broken bone. But if she pretends like nothing's wrong, if she hides behind a smile, walk on the leg anyway, eventually that brokenness would start affecting other parts of her body and it may become unrepairable. Pain was a reminder that she needs others, that no one can walk this journey alone. Pain reminded her that she's human. There's so much power in vulnerability, so why run from it just to pretend to be strong? Why hide the pain and stay in isolation? When she revealed her pain to others she was able to attract healing! She was able to create villages of support, love and common understanding. She was reminded that she is not alone. Deep down she knew not to suffer in silence when she did not have to suffer at all. God wants her pain. He'll heal her wounds if she'll let Him. She decided to trust God with her pain and He revealed people in her life she could trust with her vulnerability as well.

## I GET LOST

I get lost
I get lost in people
In search of a different me
A version of me they'll love
I get lost
I get lost in their expectations of
what a friend, a sister, a daughter,
a girlfriend, a life partner should be
I get lost
Or maybe I was never found
Maybe I never met the real me
The true version of myself
That's why I look to someone else
to show me who I should be.

# DEEP WOUNDS

I allowed you to be the band aid for
Wounds that needed stitches.
You did not break me.
I came to you in pieces.
Needing a fix and you only added to my brokenness.
It was my job to find healing, not yours.
I do not blame you for not being what I needed.

# NEVER SAYING GOODBYE

When I was eleven, I lost my cousin.
It was on a bright summer day in June.
I was anxiously waiting to get to her house
Going to see her soon.
My cousin and I were close
At least I thought so.
But to my surprise there was a lot about her I did not know.
When I arrived at my cousin's house
I didn't see her anywhere.
I greeted my aunt who said that Kim
was upset and had gone upstairs.
So, I went on my way, up those stairs to see my closest friend.
Knocked on her door, no response, so I tried to knock again.
Time went by, I grew hungry and a little confused.
She knew I was coming over but no answer,
Why did she refuse?
When her sister came by, my aunt
wondered why Kim didn't open her door.
Her absence amongst us all was growing hard to ignore.
Her sister went upstairs and started to beat down that door.
She beat. She yelled. Until the door could not hold anymore.
And when it opened, there she was, down on the floor
My cousin, my friend, breathless and limp,
had hung herself in the door.
I never understood why, but many looked to me
As if I would know,
why a 14 y.o. would decide
to let her own life go.
I was angry at her because she didn't say

she was leaving me forever.
I didn't want to believe she was gone so I told myself she wasn't.
She was my closest friend, deeper than that she was my cousin.
At her funeral, we all smiled and sang along.
No longer wanting to cry.
Convincing ourselves we're strong.
I wasn't going to say goodbye, not even to this day.
Because I know she never really left me and that she'll
Never go away.

# LONELY

I've been lonely before
Amongst friends and family
In rooms overwhelmed with laughter
And minds creating memories
I've been lonely
In your arms
I felt the distance
Your head and heart in a
different place than mine
I've felt loneliness
In the midst of everything
Going just fine.
And when I try to find the root
of my desolation nothing comes to mind.
It's like I'm in a realm of time, lost
And alone trying to find my way out of solitude.

# MEN HAVE LEFT MARKS ON ME

Long before I reached the age of understanding.
I thirst for the love and acceptance from a father
Who did not even claim me on my birth certificate.
I did not realize the marks he left on my heart until
I noticed I had an emotional deficit.
Causing me to crave love from people
even when I couldn't accept it.

And so, I may want to love you and accept your love too,
But I am struggling with my detachment and attachment issues.
That's why I push you away and act like I don't care.
That's why I start arguments over things that aren't really there.
See men have left marks on me, starting before the age of three.
They have crippled me with lies and
poisoned my thoughts with false realities...

# PHOTOGRAPHIC LOVE

I'm in love with the photos of our love.
As I sit and stare in this state of
Nostalgia because you are no longer here,
Looking at us through this photograph,
Makes me feel like you're near.
I miss you.
Reality is, we are no longer together, but
In this photo it's like we never knew that we wouldn't make it.
Happiness, a genuine happiness.
I can tell by the way my lips curled up that I was not faking.
You make me happy or should I say "made" since
Now all I have is this love inside a photograph.

# REMOTE CONTROL

Our bodies were controllers
But while I rewind to the memories of our past
you had fast forwarded to the reality of our future,
Your future, where you knew I didn't exist
And in the present, we were at the meeting point
of what was and what was going to be
And I was just hoping that you'd reconsider
changing the channel from me.

# ON BREAK-UPS

And like that, things changed.
I remember the first time I spoke your name,
Without knowing from that moment
my life wouldn't be the same.
It's crazy how now we walk pass
each other as if we are strangers,
Like we weren't just together in love and happy
talking about marriage and a one-day family
So many artifacts of our love serve
as constant reminder that we are no longer together.
You know I still have the pictures from
the mini photo shoot we had in my bathroom mirror.
That's when I realized we actually look good together.
Funny how nostalgia hits hard like an
earthquake knocking me off my balance
I'm not used to feeling this way.
Now as I remove the remnants of our love
from Instagram, Twitter, and Facebook,
I curse myself for uploading them anyway,
wondering why I ever believed in forever in the first place.
Status update...#teamsingle! It's setting in and
I'm telling myself I don't want to love again,
But of course, that's not true,
I just don't want to run into another you.
Then I start wishing that I never met you at all,
And that I never had the chance to fall because
We were supposed to walk into love anyway,
But at some point, I went too far ahead and
You got lost somewhere in between hello and goodbye.

Then, when I finally realized you were no longer by my side
It was already over between us.
And then it hits me, like the crisp wind of the morning dew,
That from the moment I gave you my heart,
I knew, that I was taking a risk.
But that's what love is about isn't it? That's what life is about.
And although it's a pain to remember your name
And to think about how everything changed,
I will fall in love over and over again,
because I know that one day a "break-up" will not be...
The End.

# I AM SAND

I am sand
Temporarily soothing
Very inviting to those
who are willing to dig deep enough.
And he loved the parts
Of me that were beautiful
The parts of me he'd only like to
Keep in a bottle to show
Off that he'd been to the beach
Traces of his presence wiped
Away from the tides of salt water
I've cried too much
Like the sand he claimed I was
Too clingy, and he didn't appreciate the way
I had managed to get into the private places,
that made him squishy and uncomfortable.
He'd build sand castles with promises
That he never had intentions of keeping,
He left them so close to the shore.
And although he'd leave me there,
left in pieces, for some reason
he'd come back wanting more

# LOVE AS YOU LOVE YOURSELF

He made it seem as if it was difficult to love her.
So, she questioned every move she'd make,
She numbered every breath she'd take.
She'd tip-toe around his insecurities and massage his ego.
She'd strip herself of her intelligence.
Pretend to be weak so that he'd feel strong
Pretend to be lost so that he could lead the way
Even if he led them into a pit of darkness she'd light
Herself on fire just to be his light.
She would stop loving herself and forget who she was
As she broke pieces of her being to add to him with
Little to no reciprocity.
She would question her beauty and forget how worthy
She was of love.
Because she loved a man without fully loving herself.

# I HOPE YOU'RE HAPPY

I wish I could text you, just to talk.
To say hey, to ask about your day.
I wonder about your thoughts (of me).
I hope you're happy and then I don't.
I kinda want you to be miserable without me.
I want you missing me so bad it aches.
I want you thinking about me while you're with her.
And you accidentally say my name.
I'm sure it isn't right for me to feel this way
but I do and...
I. don't. fucking. care.

# FAIRY TALES

Once upon a time I found a love
But that love was a lie.
I wish I could say "fuck you" and mean it
But it's been hard to just say goodbye.
I'm frustrated with my healing
I no longer want to cry
I just wish I could move forward
And stop asking or wondering why
I loved you with every piece of me
when I should've loved you whole.
Now I'm praying up to God to
remove your toxins from my soul
When you were my comfort,
I was your peace.
You said I was safe, you lied to me.
I was down for you forever
But you decided to leave
And now I'm leaning on God's promises
I want His best for me.

# PHANTOM MEMORIES

I just don't get it. I don't understand.
Why do I still miss you?
Why do I still think about the moments we shared?
Why do I think about my hands running across your beard?
Or about how you'd hide your mouth behind your hand
Whenever we FT unless you were driving.
I miss the way you looked at me with that
squint you claimed you weren't doing.
I miss hearing you say my name or bud-deeee,
Or just anything really. I miss your voice.
I miss how we'd talk in any condition: freezing cold,
sleep deprived or just for a few minutes in between time.
We'd cherish those moments and look forward to more.
I miss seeing you walk to my door, confused and unsure
Like you didn't know where to go each time,
While we cracked jokes through our phone lines.
Why do I miss this?
Why do I miss something undefined?
A brief moment in time between two people
Who did not know what they were doing.
Why do I not want to talk to you
and want to at the same time?
Why do I still want you to be mine?
Maybe part of me hopes you'd come back and change your mind.
What did you do?
Or I do?
Or we do?
Is this the power of a soul tie?
I can't seem to figure it out.

Why I want someone who couldn't choose me,
who didn't choose me?
Why I want something God removed for me?
Why do you still haunt my thoughts and even my dreams??
Lord Jesus, help me.
I'd rather just forget everything.

# #ME TOO

I remember trying to scrub traces of you off in the shower,
I must've tried for about an hour
my body went numb and my skin was red.
Heat turned into cold matching the coldness of my heart...
I wanted to forget,
to pretend that nothing happened,
I told myself I was to blame
that I shouldn't have been there.
After I refused to have sex,
after you had the audacity to take control of my body
because it was what you wanted
I still blamed me.
I walked at least 2 miles in tears,
trying to convince myself to tell someone, anyone,
but no one could be found.
I still went to work that day,
after hours of sobbing,
after losing the small piece of love I had for myself,
you made me feel worthless, like I didn't matter,
Like I was nothing,
what I wanted didn't mean anything to you
and I hated myself for making that true.
I've replayed the scene thousands of times in my head,
telling myself what I should've done instead,
but I was scared, and after I begged you to stop and you continued...
I wasn't sure what you were capable of...
So, I just laid there and just begged for you to hurry up
I cried in your bed, I felt so pathetic
And the hurting part was,

you acted like you didn't know why I was crying
I should've made you pay,
But I just pray that you've never done or never will do
what you did to me, to any other woman that comes your way.
And I know now, that I didn't deserve what you did to me.
That I'm worth more.
That I have value and purpose and strength and power within me.
You didn't take anything away from me.
I am not broken or incomplete.
I am whole.
I am WHOLE.

# ~ III ~

## ON LOVE

What is Love? She has been chasing it for so long her legs have grown tired and her heart is weak. She looked for love in the hands of lovers who would fumble her heart and walk away with less than a halfhearted apology. She searched within herself and wondered why she was unworthy of love. Why didn't her father love her? Why couldn't she love herself properly? Funny, love is her favorite word but it seems so elusive. She has been so eager to find love, she was willing to do it without God when God is Love. Fed up on her quest for romantic love she turned to God. Beaten, bruised and broken she fell to his feet begging for Him to heal her wounds. He revealed to her the greatest love she ever felt. God's love is awesome and eternal. God's love is a promise she can trust. God loves her in **every** condition. His love never fails. His love is patient, understanding, protective and forgiving. And Oh, how he Loves HER! It wasn't until she accepted Gods love that she was able to start loving herself. If this God of everything could love her in all her imperfections, who was she to say she's unworthy when He says she is worthy? After she had her son she began to understand God's love a lot better. Her son is her heart in human form, he's an extension of her. The love she has for him is unconditional. Even when she disciplines him or set boundaries it's because she loves him **carefully** and she wants to protect him from getting hurt. She allows him to explore and test his limits with a watchful eye. She affirms him even when he frustrates her or make mistakes. He's her creation, made in the image of her. She loves him as God loves her.

Heavenly Father,
Thank you for loving me *carefully.*
-Her

# FOR KEZIAH

Black bodies birthing black bodies.
Creating life produced by love.
Evolving from seeds
Sprouting roots of royalty,
power, melanin, creativity
to the fibers of your being.
There is a being growing inside of me
And my heart will soon be
manifested into human form.

For you I will...
And I always will...

Thank you for allowing me to love you.
Thank you for pushing me into
Being the best version of myself for you.
I have never had a love like this and
I thank God for this blessing.
I pray for God's guidance to lead you to
Becoming the man, He envisioned,
when He formed you in my womb.

# DEAR SISTER

You have been a blessing
from the moment you entered the room,
fresh out the womb I held you in my little palms
and I knew there was a God.
I prayed for you, I told God I'd be
the best big sister I could be and
I hope you believe that I am
You have been the best sister anyone could ask for.
You have been the best friend.
Your heart is big and pure as Gold
the way it shines for the world
Girl you shine...so bright like the sun.
You are radiant and beautiful and amazing and
authentic and supportive and confident and strong,
and the list could go on and on.
I love you.
You're like an annoying song
that continues to play in your head
but it's so good and catchy
you still turn it up when it comes on.
You are magic.
A breath of fresh air.
Never pretending, always understanding and
willing to stand up or step in for those you love.
I admire you. I affirm you. I adore you.
And I am so honored to be
connected to who God is creating you to be.
My sister, a young queen!
Reign...with your head held high,

never forgetting your crown, standing in your anointing,
Reign in forgiveness and belief in yourself.
Reign, knowing that you have kingdom in you
and God's power running through you.
Reign in love and in peace and in joy.
You deserve it all sis!
And I thank God for the many years
he’s given me with you.
And I pray that his provision continues...

## SOUND

I did not ask to be a part of your symphony
But your conduction carried me in anyway,
Playing the strings of my harp to create a sound you found pleasing,
Manipulating the rhythm of my personal song,
Losing it as I am infusing into a harmony of us,
A harmony of trust, a harmony of passion, a harmony of love.
I'm scared.
But I'm not sure where that fear stems from.
So, I zone out, listening to the sound.
The sound of music. Your voice is music to my...
Sound of peace. I find peace in your...
Sound of love. Your love is driving me crazy.
And the sound of your heartbeat,
Your love is always on my mind.
Reminding me that you're still conducting this symphony.
And maybe the reason I am so afraid is because
I don't have much control of this journey
Of movements, of sound, of our story;
And for the longest I've only been playing to my own beat.
So, when you started to play your piece,
I didn't expect you to know the right keys.
See, I did not ask to be a part of your symphony
But your conduction carried me in anyway.

# A LOVE WORTH FIGHTING FOR

He was a breath of fresh air
Able to take me out of my element
When I'm usually in my head
But he had a passageway to my thoughts
And nothing about this was easy
He showed me the challenges of love
And made me realize that
this is how love supposed to be
Something worth fighting for.

# GUARDED

He stripped me naked
Pulling back the layers
Of protection I had in place
In order to feel secure
I wasn't ready to be wrapped
In the blanket of his arms
His arms were weapons to me
So, I remain guarded
Missiles locked, ready to defend
my head and my heart
But even they were at war somctimes
My head telling me to leave
My heart saying
His arms are where love is
But I couldn't trust that he wouldn't
Hold on too tightly or not tight enough
And to make decisions just
based off of feelings were not enough
Because I've known from experience
that my heart was not to be trusted
And my head was never sure
Of what it wanted.

# HOLD ME

I want you to hold me,
Without fear
But with understanding,
That you have found
Someone sacred.
A woman,
Who embodies the essence
And light of God.
Who is Gods temple.
A Queen, noble in character
With an inheritance that
assures her and you,
of her worth, value and authenticity.
Hold me with respect, confidence
love, courage and boldness.
Hold me with faith in your heart
And confirmation in your fingertips.
Hold me.
But by all means
Do not hold me out
of fear of losing me
Or out of uncertainty
Of when our last days will be.
Hold me knowing that the Lord
has directed our paths together
If not to stay forever,
Then for a reason or a season
But either way
At least we've held on to

One another as precious
Gifts from our father.

# TO MY FUTURE HUSBAND

I'd write a poem about you
Beginning and ending with love
I'd write about the God in you
Connecting to the God in me
Ordained by the heavens above
I'd write your name in 1 Corinthians 13
Verses 4-8 instead of the word love I'd write you
and I know it'll still relate.
I'd write of our power and our faith
And the vision of love, we wish to create
With and through each other
I'd write a poem about how we walked into love,
After walking into alignment,
after walking in obedience
after walking by faith that God
would have the best for me and
you are the best blessing that
I believe would come true.
I'd write a poem about you
And it'll read of love too.

# MOTHER NATURE'S FLOW

I looked upon a starless sky with a moon that was hard to find,
I was led by his light.
A guiding touch through her throne of trees,
bed of rocks and waterfalls.
There was safety in his arms and security in his voice.
I was calm.
And I wondered about romance,
Questioning if this is what love feels like.
The coldness in the air was blanketed by
The warmth of our bodies.
He pulled me close,
I closed my eyes and listened to the waterfall.
He kissed my lips and my neck.
His hands traced the goosebumps
down my back then my waters began to fall.
And I wondered if this is what love feels like.
Waters rushing, temperatures rising,
Moans being carried away by whistling winds.
I wasn't ready to go with the flow; the current was too fast.
Mother Nature was making moves within my body
but I had to go against her authority,
even though I had been seduced
by the beauty of her Queendom.
I decided to be still with him.
And to just listen to the waterfall
Knowing that we had plenty of time
to discover what love feels like.

# 1 CORINTHIANS 13:4-8

I've found love
in every word of affirmation you speak towards me
I find love in your whispers
When you speak of a life together for eternity
I feel love with every breath, with every touch,
with every kiss I share with you
I feel it, when I prefer you over oxygen.
I'd suffocate in you,
because close never feels close enough
So, don't you ever leave my side and
I know that there's no fear in love
but I'm afraid of the day that we ever have to part
so, I pray that in your presence I'll stay always.
It's crazy how I could never get tired of looking at you,
and as I stare into the depths of your eyes,
I realize it is there that I reside,
So, thank you, thank you for allowing me to truly see you,
and not just the surface level, shallow version of the truth
but the real, unadulterated, imperfectly created marvelous,
and wonderfully made version of you.
And thank you for trusting me with your heart,
your soul and most importantly your time,
for every moment we share is one
we can never get back and I'm blessed
that you found me worthy of that.
Even though I wasn't sure that I was ready
to feel love again when you asked me...
my brokenness almost kept me from my blessing.
It had me believe that I would never find love again,

that I wasn't worthy of you that you were not worthy of me
but love always perseveres and I was healed
scars and wounds began to disappear
when you show me what love really is.
And you show me what love really is on the daily,
Love is patient,
and you've waited until I got out of my own way to allow you in
Love is kind,
and I am grateful for a man who gives so much
to the world and still shows me he's mine
Love is not boastful or jealous or proud or rude
And you are modest and trusting and humble and polite.
See I know that God lives within you because
you've shown me what love is and love is you.

# GOD'S LOVE

It felt good to be seen
Not just in pieces
Not in someone else's expectations
of who she was supposed to be
Not as her mistakes or her shortcomings
He saw her whole, complete.
He went right through her veil of lies and insecurities
and he found her sweet spot
He found her deep
Beyond the mask she wore for the world
Beyond the broken promises she told herself
Beyond what the naked eye could see
She could finally be seen
And for the first time in her life she was no longer hiding.

## ~ IV ~

## ON FAITH

For many years she struggled with having faith. She struggled because faith required her to relinquish control and she was too busy trying to be her own God and control everything. She questioned her faith because she wasn't sure if it was truly hers or her Grandmother's or her mother's. Did she know God for herself? If not, how could she have faith in Him? It wasn't until her own encounter with God that she felt a stirring in her spirit and the seed of faith that her mother and grandmother planted in her was watered. Her faith in God began to grow when she was struggling with depression and feelings of worthlessness. Her faith grew when she was tired of feeling empty and disposable. Her faith grew when she decided to leave her pain on a church altar in Japan and she felt the spirit of God hug her. Her faith grew when she decided to walk away from what was comfortable into isolation and uncertainty. Her faith grew and continues to grow. As she becomes the woman God created her to be, her faith has become more radical and crazy. She's trusting God in ways she never has before. She's relinquishing control and believing in His promises. She's learning to choose His will over hers. She's accepting His truths over the lies of her "inner me." Although it has been a process and she has fallen short countless times, her faith defeated the countless lies of the enemy and reminds her that God truly loves her! Her faith carries her into oceans too deep her feet may fail but she knows a God who would never let her drown.

## PLEASURE WITHOUT PEACE

He was my method of escape.
And we would invade
each other's fantasies, forgetting reality
We'd find pleasure.
Misleading our hearts into believing that
this indulgence was okay
because it felt good.
But what's good isn't always what's right.
We didn't have faith so we were led by sight.
Afraid that we were too out of touch to receive God's best
we fell victim to the desires of our flesh,
And we found pleasure.
Pleasure in our codependency.
It felt good to be needed,
Filling pieces and mending hearts
to our best ability not realizing
that it was ourselves we were emptying,
pouring into each other but still
remaining half full.
He was my God, at least that's
what I made him and
I was ashamed to admit that I wanted
him to fill voids and be the source of my strength,
as if he was omnipotent.
He was not.
And I was at fault for setting those expectations
But when I was in his arms
I found pleasure, connectedness to him,
a man of many faces, the same relationships,

just multiple embraces.
I'd fallen short and I felt it in my spirit.
So, engulfed in the darkness
my light began to diminishes.
But... I had found pleasure...
a pleasure without peace because
my spirit was dis-eased and
my heart infected with disease.
I felt broken
and this time I knew
no man could mend the pieces.
So, I decided to consult with the source
of my existence.
Realizing, I should've done *that* to begin with.

# TO MR. DISTRACTION

I risked so much of myself for you,
while you didn't give anything at all.
Losing pieces of me
each time I chose to please you over God.
I submitted my love to you thinking you would appreciate it,
Given how much it cost me.
But you were only there to receive not caring about my feelings.
I was willing to die for you, because you said you couldn't breathe
So, I lent you my lungs and when your heart was broken,
I gave you mine, along with a soothing touch.
I really didn't ask for much
but I expected you to at least, be considerate
And you weren't so now I am stuck, here, with my damage.
I can't believe I let you be the reason
why I couldn't be closer to God.
Why I couldn't give myself wholeheartedly,
my mind AND my body, because
I knew it would inconvenience you
since I had shared those with you already.
Even without you putting in enough love,
enough work and enough of yourself
I was risking it all for you.
I sinned with you.
I lied for you.
I died repeatedly for you,
And for the thought of us
Because the thought of not having you at the time,
Was a lot scarier than disappointing God.

I was foolish for you.
I was careless for you.
I risked it all...for you.
So much of myself I was willing to lose to please you
and, in the end, ...
You were NEVER worth it!

# MISPERCEPTION

Caught up in her misperception that she is an exception to his rule,
she laid there wide open, releasing herself unto him.
Thinking they were so much more she disclosed her
deepest thoughts to him and laid there bare.
She allowed herself to be vulnerable in front of him.
Thinking that he was doing the same, when he caressed her frame
and showed her his sensitive side.
So, she laid there releasing herself open wide.
Now as he walks out the door his needs fulfilled
she wonders why he can't love her.
Arms crossed over her body
she wraps her nakedness under her covers.
His needs were pleased and although she reached her peak
she needed so much more than what he was willing to offer.
But she let him back in, submitting to his advances,
she released herself unto him again.
His feelings hadn't change still
And he looks at her and asks what's the big deal?
He tells her she knew what she was getting into
And that they were just kickin' it and just cool.
See, he wasn't looking for love and
she wasn't looking to be loved at first
but she was deceived by what she perceived
to be inside of him which was more than lust
and a desire to be taken into a different dimension of passion.
Displeased at the outcome of this she discarded him
As her lover and friend and went on her path of transformation.
She didn't need his love like she thought and she didn't need him.
Although she struggled with her misperception

of love she no longer released herself to anyone
who only provided her with a crippled reflection.
Finally, she recognizes herself as a Queen only to be treated like so
no longer accepting the no calls and no shows.
Finally, she gave her heart to God, the one who truly cares,
and she no longer has to make her own assumptions.
He loves her inside and out, nothing to perceive and no doubts
This is the end to her misperceptions.

# RETURNED

Forgive me Lord, because I almost forgot who I belonged to.
And last night I said some things I wasn't supposed to,
and I did some things too.
Forgetting that I belong to a King that has
placed me above those things so I had no business...
And I don't know why I struggle so hard with
Ignoring the desires of my flesh, since, in my heart you reside.
So, everything I do or say should resemble you.
But it's like I'm so comfortable with lies,
I've started to resent the truth.
You know what scares me?
You returning, and not recognizing me.
I wonder if you would see the light of you in me
Or if I'll just blend into the darkness of my society.
Nah, I won't let that be the case.
I am covered by your mercy and amazing grace and
I appreciate that you haven't given up on me already,
Although I couldn't blame you if you did.
But I know you're still working on me
And I know I can be better once I quit making excuses.
So, forgive me Father, I have sinned.
Your daughter recognizes that she needs you.
Without me accepting your love I'm incomplete.
I want to be whole. And my destiny needs me to be.
Feed me with your word, so I can embody
Your integrity, your righteousness, your strength.
So that I can finally forgive myself and release all shame.
And I'll finally be able to love myself again.
Thank You! Thank you!

Thank you for giving me another chance,

And I declare on "This" day, I will not leave out the same way I came.

# RELEASING FEAR

I'd say see you later but part of me hopes that's not the case.
The part of me that believes
I'd still have some form of attachment lingering,
I guess.
However, see you later sounds better than goodbye
and I said I wasn't saying that again.
There's hope in "see you later"'
and I guess there is "good" in goodbye,
I know this one is good, great really...for me, and I hope for you too.
I remember asking "what am I holding onto?"
And I've realized, after all this time, it's been fear.
Fear that I wouldn't find someone who could make me
laugh, smile, think, *orgasm,* or inspire more creativity like you do.
Fear that I won't feel desired, no one would be "thirsty" for me,
or they won't be grateful and thank me
for even the shortest time they get to spend with me.
Fear that I won't feel special, interesting or fully appreciated.
Fear that another "He" won't look at me as a masterpiece and say
"You don't need to change a damn thing."
Fear that my feelings won't be heard or validated.
Fear that I could easily be forgotten or left behind or disregarded.
Fear that I am disposable, not worthy of love or true commitment
Fear that I'm alone and that I always will be.
See I wasn't really holding on to you,
like I thought...although for you I am grateful.
You showed me a glimpse of the man God has for me,
A glimpse of the type of connection I will have with him.
A glimpse of how he will make me feel. But that's it, just a glimpse.
The man God has for ME is out there.

And I will NOT have to share.
He does exist and I know despite how I may feel about you,
YOU ARE NOT IT.
And I will not settle for just what I can get.
I won't have to question my position in his life because he'll know.
He will be decisive and intentional with me.
So, in saying goodbye to you,
I'm releasing all the fears I've been holding on to.
I am believing in abundance,
accepting everything that is rightfully MINE
and releasing what isn't, starting with **you.**

# CLOSER

I can feel the tugging on my heart to draw closer.
So close that there will be no space for insecurities,
No space for uncertainty, no space for loneliness,
No space for unrighteousness, and no space for fear.
I can feel God and the time is near, when I move forward
In my walk with Him, letting go of doubt and shame,
Living my life in HIS name.
I want to get close, closer than I've ever been.

# F.E.A.R

False evidence appearing real.
It's amazing how something that doesn't really exist
holds so much power.
We will let the idea of something bad happening,
limit opportunities that can be ours.
And after hours of waiting, contemplating and
hesitating we let it hold us back,
We let it stop us from making the move.
Then soon, we lose.
Because the opportunity to do something
we would love to pursue has expired.
So, we exhaust our doubts and our ambition runs tired
And exhausted from chasing the pipe dreams of nice things,
This life seems to be one big ol' test,
Given to teach before we have even learned the lesson.
So, we get caught up in our own inhibitions
suppressing our true desires.
Which burn like fire but watered down, we seem to drown,
Caught up in the real world,
stressed when our walls are coming down,
Around us, the trouble we didn't want surrounds us,
but help from on high astounds us,
Because it seems the Lord has found us.
And in the Lord, we find trust.
And we understand, we need faith,
because fear cannot prevail where faith resides.

# LET GO. LET GOD...

I found peace
In my heart
I found freedom
In my mind
I found trust
In what's next
Once I decided
To let go
And let God.

# NAKED

I remember when I allowed
Him to see me naked
To my surprise I felt no shame.
Covered by His peace
I realized I never felt freer.
I was completely bare,
withholding nothing.

# RELATIONS WITH SIN

When we first met
You promised me
An eternity of pleasure
Of life fully lived
Of unforgettable memories
Of living without regrets
You promised
That I could have everything
That I could have anything
That I'd feel free
That I'd be complete
Indulging into my flesh
Allowing the world to consume me
For it to direct my paths and lead
Me to prosperity
I'd find success
In you, with you, by you.
I just needed to give in
So, I let go and let sin
Stir up the wickedness
in my heart
Then my desires had start
To work against me,
And I found shame
I found brokenness
And emptiness
And chaos
I fought myself
I resented my flesh

I had nothing
I thought I lost everything
I was no longer living
You were crippling
To my spirit
To my peace
To my destiny
You promised lies
That I swallowed
down with
bread and wine
Trying to revitalize
The me within
That was so consumed
With the pleasures of
Being in bed with sin.
But God.
He taught me
how to forgive myself
He showered me with grace
And mercy
He gave me Jesus
So, I no longer make
Provisions for you.
I've learned to let go
Building my trust in Him
I got to know peace
Everlasting joy,
I accepted abundance
And I found love
Real, undeniable love
The love of God
And through the power
of His love,
I learned how to love

Myself better
Than I ever
did when I was with you.

# MY PRAYER CLOSET

This is the place where I find refuge
The place where I seek, where I cry out,
where I sing, where I dance, where I shout,
where I praise, where I worship.
This is a place of war and surrender
Of breaking and healing
Toe to toe I stand against myself
I will not leave out the same way I came
This is the place where demons are slain
Where freedom and victory reigns
No more bondage, no more chains
This is the place where the old me dies
And the new me rise
This is the place of coronation
The place where I learn to balance
the weight of my C.R.O.W.N.
This is the place where I accept my inheritance
and I rebuke the lies of the adversary.
This is the place of releasing and receiving
The place of vulnerability and weakness
Of encouragement and strength
Where I learn to forgive myself and others
This is the place where I rebuke generational curses
Where I step into purpose,
walk in my anointing,
And turn my mess into my ministry,
This is the place of liberty.
This is the place of identity.
I don't just show up for me but for everyone attached to my destiny.

This is the place of *becoming.*

## ~ V ~

## ON BECOMING

As I stare at her in the mirror I see me smiling back at me. I worry about her and who she is becoming. As I pray for her, I pray for me. For I am Her and she is me.

The idea of becoming was a new concept I heard while attending a church in LA 5 years ago. I'd never thought of my journey as becoming anything, I just was who I was, at least that's what I thought. The Oxford definition of becoming is "the process of coming to be something or of passing into a state." After hearing this concept, I wondered two things: who am I becoming? And who am I now? I learned that in the process of coming to be something I had to accept who I was and who I am presently. That has truly been a struggle because I had never loved the person I was and I've been struggling to accept the person I am therefore, the woman I want to become seems like a fantasy. However, I've chosen to believe the prophetic words of my pastor, that "I am a woman becoming." I am continuously evolving and passing in to a state of renewal and transformation. I am becoming whole. I am becoming free. I am becoming confident. I am becoming powerful through my vulnerability. I am becoming a leader. I am becoming the highest version of myself. I am becoming authentic. I am becoming healed. I am becoming mentally, spiritually, physically and emotionally stronger. I am becoming the me God envisioned before I was formed in my mother's womb. And yes, it is and has been a challenging yet rewarding process, filled with tears, broken hearts, love, transitions, laughter, loss and pain but I've become stronger along the way. I am a woman becoming and I'm learning to love **her**...properly.

To DaQuala Shabri Hunt:

I am proud of who you were, who you are and who you are becoming. I love and choose you daily.

-You, Me, Her

# BREAK-UP WITH SELF

I never knew how to be with you,
I know that's messed up to say
Sometimes you'd be so negative
or you'd let other people get in our way
I really wanted to love you but you couldn't accept me as I am,
Nit-picky and controlling, you always wanted me to change.
I was either too fat to be sexy
Too dumb to say anything
I never felt worthy
All you did was complain
You wanted things to be different
Better than before
You wanted to be greater
You needed to love yourself more.
So, you pushed me away,
And I was led astray,
to men who claimed
That they could make me happy
That they could ease my pain,
I broke up with you so many times
Looking for someone else
to make me whole.
I was looking for completion,
looking for the happiness
someone stole.
But when it was all said and done,
I realized I could no longer run.
And in order to move forward,
It was you I had to confront.

I had to stop judging you for
who you weren't ready to be,
I had to forgive you for your mistakes
And your short comings
I had to learn how to love you,
And accept that you
still had room to grow
I had learned to affirm you
Assuring you that you're
Worth getting to know.
There was more to you
than I was able to see
So, I learned how to be with you
Because after all you are me.

# THIS SKIN

This skin was not always easy to love
When the world continued to give me reasons to hate it.
But after 27 years of perfecting self-love
I am honored to embrace it
My body, God's temple,
an inheritance of rubies that people like to imitate,
but only God could create
Only the worthy could relate
Its rarity to royalty,
My inheritance to nobility
I am a beautiful black Queen
Proud to be in my skin
Proud to be in this body.

# QUIET STORM

I am still waters
But there's something raging inside of me
An internal storm
Of chaos and peace
Of destruction and creativity,
Of life and death
Of love and hate
Let me flow, freely
Into rivers, oceans, waterfalls and streams
Let me rage, freely
Into crashing waves, hurricanes and tsunamis
I can't always be still.
I can't always be peace.

## WOMAN, LOVE YOU

I want you to love you
Just for the sake of loving you
Not because it will prepare
you for loving another
but because you deserve to be loved.
You deserve to know love for yourself.
From yourself.
By yourself.

# THE TRUTH

MY beauty is not determined by society's lies,
so, I will no longer partake in them.
MY truth is in my roots
that spring out of me vibrantly.
It's in the shade of my skin
that makes me uniquely designed
combined with what's within.
It's in my smile and the versatility of my hair
because my beauty is flexible
and I can bend but NEVER be broken.
MY beauty is strong and divine.
My beauty is MINE,
And no longer defined by society
or men who can't understand
that my curves are meant to be loved,
my smile is meant to be adorned,
my lips are meant to be full, of love and laughter,
and MY beauty is far from what you see.
I have redefined what beauty is and beauty is naturally ME.

# PRESSURE

Pressure piling on like traffic,
Irritating like white noise, it's static,
pushing me to be something more.
Something else besides myself
and it cause me to be beside myself
as I gain control of the wheel I decide to
let go of fear so that God can take the lead,
driving me to who the pressure is making me to be,
I'm developing, and it's on, game plan
no more talking I'm coming with action,
no more relaxing...just stacking,
doing more than just making it,
I'm shaking this, a change maker, a game changer,
using my voice to spread the truth,
to shine my light, to brighten the sky,
I stay lit, I stay fit mentally
stretching my understanding no more romancing reality,
keeping it 100 even when it feels like sense and
you just want to forget,
wanting to stop feeling dismissed and left behind,
like we don't matter but we come back stronger,
yes we come back better, the pressure is on and we need it,
to mold and to forge us, make us legit,
the purest version of ourselves
no longer processed to the conformity of the ages
who would rather keep us asleep in the low levels of consciousness
Are you conscious yet?
How can you be asleep when the world needs you?
Be spiritually awake so that you can be used.

See, your life is not just for you,
Yet you distract yourself and disregard
the God given gifts that qualify you.
Which leads me to one last thing to say,
make sure you don't waste your gifts today.

# GRIND IN ME

I'm looking for the grind in me
That persevering, never quitting, motivating energy
But it's like when the road gets rough
I lose my tough and my knees begin to buckle up.
My mind begins to wander, thoughts of failing,
not prevailing and everything begins to feel bigger than me.
Then I think that maybe this dream, this path,
this goal is not meant to be.
Or Maybe just maybe this part of my journey
isn't needed to fulfill my destiny.
I quit.
Then I sit, uneasy, still deprived of peace, because I knew
quitting was never an answer.
Realizing, that nothing worth having is easy
and if I want it easy, then I don't deserve it anyway.
I understand now that God wants to see
how much I'm willing to sacrifice,
how much I'm willing to put in, in order to live purposefully.
See he wasn't playing games when he created me.
I was created with precision and intention
and after 27 years he is still on the mission
of molding me into the woman he created me to be.
So, know that...everything takes time, and it will not be easy
but I guarantee it'll be worth it.

# QUEEN

Queen,
Where is your crown?
You've left it behind in the midst of feeling down,
Of feeling bound by misrepresentations
and low expectations of who you are.
Constantly consuming messages from mainstream that
you should aspire to be a "bad bitch"
Sharing booty shots and half naked pics,
as if "likes" can increase your value.
And there are people in this world
that benefits from your insecurities,
They benefit from you not knowing your worth
or knowing that you are royalty.
And trust me, You. Are. Royalty.

Queen,
You are beautifully made.
The creator knew exactly what he was doing
When he blessed you with a head full of vibrant curls,
When he gave you lips full of life, hips of endurance,
the graceful curves of your thighs
And that skin, that immaculate skin full of melanin.
Love the skin that you're in, even if no one else does.
And the most incredible thing He gave you was your voice.
Given to be spoken with confidence and silent when needed.
Given to heal the injured and uplift the weakened.
Given to speak truth and to teach
young kings and queens that they have POWER.
Power in their hearts.

Power in their minds.
Power in their hands.
Power in their voice.

Queen,
You are the essence of life birthing new generations
And leaving an empowering legacy.
Never forget the ones who paved the way for you.
The Ida B. Well's, Maya Angelou's and Sojourner Truth's.
They did all they could to make things better for you.
Be bold. Be brave.
As you walk in the footsteps of the Queens
Who sacrificed and laid down their lives
So that our generation can do more than just breathe,
Remember to believe.
Believe in your capabilities and
Be ready to fight for your Queendom.
My sister, My Queen,
Always remember that
Your black is beautiful,
Your black is strong,
Your black is wisdom,
Your black is indestructible.
Your black is magic
Your black is yours.
No one can ever take that away from you
Because your black is a gift from God.
Embrace all that you are, sit on your thrown,
NEVER forget your C.R.O.W.N,
Then watch as the world around you
Bows down.

# LIGHT OUT OF DARKNESS

I was born into darkness
I struggled to see the light
At the end of the tunnel, it was me.
But I was afraid to look inside
Afraid that I would see the darkness
creeping inside of me.
There was none.
And I realized my luminescence
Prove that it's not where you come from that matters
It's who you choose to be in spite of it.
I chose to be light.

# YOU CAN'T AFFORD THE WOMAN I AM NOW

You cannot afford the woman I am now
All that I had to offer, I've given
Sometimes more than I should have
But I've grown a lot smarter
And so much wiser
I can't give more chances than deserved
My heart is worth more
**I'm worth more.**
No more discounts so don't ask
Because...

You cannot afford the woman I am now
You thought what you were giving was love
Love it was not
No sense of selflessness, no sacrifice
Self-serving and full of it you were.
And I thought that I couldn't find better than you
How foolish I was to believe
You convinced me you were the best I ever had
A lie you had the audacity to conceive
You used to say that I'd never let you go
And at the time you may have been right
My insecurities kept me glued and blind
But now I've regained my sight
And I know that...

You could never afford me, not even then.
Although I was whipped by the D, love had me under a spell

Lust had me in a trance and your mouth piece
Had me speechless
You still didn't deserve me!
I was always worth more
But you were given too much power
And definitely **too much credit**
Now you've reached your limit, completely maxed out.
So, believe me when I say...
**you cannot afford the woman I am now.**

# I AM

I have believed many lies that have led me
away from who I am. **That ends today**!
I'm no longer being defined by my hurt or my pain.
I am believing in my heart and meditating on God's truth
And He says:

I am strong.
I am enough.
I am loved.
I am lovable.
I am a conqueror.
I am victorious.
I am chosen.
I am qualified.
I am wise.
I am intelligent.
I am an inspiration.
I am a Queen.
I am a blessing.
I am gifted.
I am creative.
I am a healer.
I am healed.
I am more.
I am worthy.
I am equipped.
I am royalty.
I am a Kingdom Woman.
I am God's heir.

I am a believer.
I am an overcomer.
I am whole.
I am complete.
I am a deliverer.
I am delivered.
I am a forgiver.
I am forgiven.
I am God's workmanship.
I am who God says I am.
I am a masterpiece.
I am Beautiful.
I am at peace.
I am
***Me.***

# DEAR DAQUALA SHABRI HUNT,

I have one good question for you but before you answer, I want you to really think are you answering for you or for someone else? My question is: what do you want to do with your life to bring true happiness and fulfillment? Now, with that answer, what are you going to do about it? You've always wanted to lead a life where you're doing what you love. So seize the opportunities to follow your heart and fulfill your dreams. Leave F.E.A.R behind and doubt at the door. This dream has been placed in you for a reason, own up to it! Speak it into existence, allow God to manifest it and expect it to come into fruition. God has placed these gifts in you for a reason and you cannot go anywhere without them coming out of you. They cannot be hidden, so don't allow them to be. It's time to take action and stop making excuses. You got this! There's nothing to it but to do it, so get it done! Fight off insecurities that tell you that you are inadequate, not capable, that it's not for you, that you won't be successful, or that people would not support you. Remember that God is always for you and that he has ordained you to be victorious. He has plans to prosper you and to give you a future and a hope. He has given you the ability to create in many ways so take heed and do it for His glory. When you get to the end of your life, I pray that you look back without "what ifs?" I pray that when you die, you die empty because you created all the things you wished to create. I pray that you will not contribute to the other riches that live in the graves of untapped potential, lost visions and forgotten dreams. Stop being afraid of the woman you're becoming, She. Is. Amazing.

-HER

# ACKNOWLEDGEMENTS

Thank you to GOD for your grace, love, mercy and the ability to create. Thank you Keziah for being the number one reason why I wish to be and do better. Thank you to my family and friends for continuing to support me and for creating a space where I can trust you with my vulnerabilities. Thank you for being my village. Thank you mom for your unwavering support, for writing my foreword and for giving me your tenacity, boldness and resilience. Thank you, Chloe, for being my faith building partner, you were the first person to show me what crazy faith looks like (homeless in LA days lol). Thank you to my readers and supporters, you allow my voice to be heard. To the "men" who have contributed to my growth, my happiness, my pain and the therapeutic escape of my pen, thank you for the experiences that we shared. Special thanks to Amber, for lending a hand and being willing to share knowledge to help another author, I appreciate you. Thank you, CJ, for taking my beautiful picture and for always pushing me to think BIGGER and share my gifts with the world. Thank you, Brie, for your contribution to my copyright and for always being ready to support any of my ideas since day one, you continue to gas me up and tell me how capable I am. Once again, thank you everyone who made this investment in me, I hope that it was not only a good read but also touched and inspired you in some way!

-Peace, Love, and Everlasting joy y'all!

www.ingramcontent.com/pod-product-compliance
Ingram Content Group UK Ltd.
Pitfield, Milton Keynes, MK11 3LW, UK
UKHW041641190726
13854UKWH00006B/2631